# Make Do & Mend

# Make Do & Mend

## Katie Ebben

PHOTOGRAPHY BY CHRIS TUBBS

conran OCTOPUS

First published in 2005 by Conran Octopus Limited
a part of Octopus Publishing Group
2–4 Heron Quays, London E14 4JP
www.conran-octopus.co.uk

British Library Cataloguing-in-Publication Data.
A catalogue record for this book is available from the British Library.

ISBN 1 84091 425 4
Printed in China

Publishing Director: Lorraine Dickey
Art Directors: Lucy Gowans and Jonathan Christie
Executive Editor: Zia Mattocks
Designer: Nicky Barneby
Editor: Siobhán O'Connor
Illustrator: Alice Tait
Stylist: Katie Ebben
Photographer's Assistant: Natasha Sturny
Production Manager: Angela Couchman

# Contents

# Introduction

With clothing retailers churning out cheap new designs fortnightly and the term 'throwaway fashion' in common usage, you may well ask what need there is for a book called *Make Do & Mend*. And since we are on the subject, you are probably also questioning whether it has any relevance to the way we live today. After all, isn't 'making do' an outdated concept and something our grandparents or even our great-grandparents did only out of necessity?

But making do and mending aren't all about living a miserable existence of scrimping and saving. Their primary focus is more about taking a creative and resourceful approach to life, learning to recycle your possessions and not discarding them until they really have outlived their usefulness. It's the opposite of dashing out to buy a new pair of trousers and tossing the old ones away because they have holes in the knees or the seam has ripped or, worse, they are simply no longer fashionable. It's about finding reinvented life in a slightly tired or dated item that still has plenty of wear left in it given a bit of creative attention and a stitch in time.

I'm definitely not suggesting that you stay in every night to darn the holes in your socks (if they're cotton, use them for polishing the furniture or buffing your shoes) or that you walk around dressed in dowdy hand-me-downs – where is the joy in that? But creating, for example, a corsage to hide a snag in your jumper means you make something both pretty and practical, and aren't adding to the mountains of waste in a throwaway society.

Making do and mending do mean that you will need to invest some of that most precious commodity – time. These days we all feel we don't have enough of it, so try to view time spent being creative as 'you time', rather than as a chore. Listen to some music while you're at it, and remind yourself that making things is a rewarding activity.

It is best to keep your projects simple in the beginning. This way you avoid becoming bored and giving up on a design that is too ambitious. My early attempts at sewing and making are littered with unfinished projects that were beyond my abilities or required more time than I had patience for – the crocheted top being a memorable non-starter that hung around in unfinished bits for years. And if you're still not persuaded to change your mind-set and flex your sewing skills, then think of your pocket – ultimately it costs less to repair and reinvent than it does to buy a brand-new replacement. But don't give yourself a hard time about the odd shopping spree because nothing lasts for ever and sometimes you just can't beat the thrill of having something new to use or wear.

Remember, life is full of stuff and it's worth looking after the things you love.

Trimming

# All the Trimmings

There is nothing so effective as a bit of nifty trimming to transform the most boring article of clothing or household item, but use it as a decorative weapon with a degree of caution – as with eating cake, too much of a good thing can be bad. It's best to avoid having your home or, worse, yourself looking over the top 'tasseltastic' and dressed for Christmas all year round. Remember that trimming is not only an ornamental tool, but has a functional purpose, too, and can be used to disguise joins, seams, raw edges or even a row of tacks on upholstery.

# Types of Trimming

**WELT** (or piping) is a band of fabric usually wrapped around a cord, which is then sewn into a seam to create a piped edge, and is used a lot on upholstery and around the edges of cushions to give a neat tailored look. For a subtle effect, use it in the same colour as the main fabric; for a more defined result, use a contrasting colour. For example, a chair upholstered in grey linen with a black piped edge will look ultra-smart and quite formal.

**TASSELS** are most easily described as dangling ornaments made from a bunch of loose threads gathered together at the top. They can be used to adorn just about everything from cushions to door keys and curtains or drapes. They come in a fantastic range of colours, sizes and materials, with prices to match.

**CORD** is kind of like decorative rope. It is made up from strands of fibre – often in contrasting colours and different thicknesses – twisted together to make a single cord. A more elaborate version of welt, cord is often used for the same purposes, but its fancy appearance means it doesn't need covering in fabric first.

**BRAID** is commonly made from three (sometimes more) strands of welting covered in fabric, which are then braided together. You're quite likely to find it swagged and stitched around the soft furnishings of traditionally inspired interiors. Like cord and welt, it is used to define the edges of seams.

**FRINGE** was greatly loved by the Victorians and also used in abundance on the flapper dresses of the Roaring Twenties. It usually has a narrow decorative band from which loose strands of fibre hang. It comes in countless numbers of colours, lengths and materials. (See how we have used fringing in the project on page 13.)

**RUFFLE** is a rather girlie trim and is usually a shirred or gathered edge made from fabric. You will often find it used as a pretty border for cushions, skirts and tops, and occasionally (but not always advisedly) on curtains and sofas.

**FLANGE** may have an off-putting name, but ignore this. It is the simplest-looking of the border trims, as it is basically a flat piece of fabric used for edging. Flange is most commonly seen on sofas and sometimes includes a pleat in the centre.

**RIBBON** comes in all sorts of forms – satin and taffeta, velvet, sheer, jacquard, grosgrain, braided, metallic, wire-edged, pleated and frilled. There really is a ribbon for everything. And it can be used to trim a multitude of things, from clothes to soft furnishings, in a multitude of ways. (For example, see how we have used ribbon on pages 14 and 17.)

# Make your own Tassels

1. Cut a rectangular piece of card slightly wider than the length you want your tassel to be.

2. Wrap silk thread or wool around the card until you have wound a good amount on to make a chunky tassel.

3. Slip a double length of cord under the threads at one end of the card. Tie the cord securely to hold the threads together. This is now the top end of the tassel.

4. Hold the top end of the tassel firmly in your hand and, using a pair of scissors, snip along the bottom edge (the opposite edge to where you have tied the threads together). Discard the card.

5. To create the neck of the tassel, take a length of thread, make a loop and hold it against the tassel, a little bit down from the top. Wrap the other end of thread around the tassel to bind all the loose threads together. Then slip the free end of your binding thread through the loop and pull it tight to secure.

6. Snip the thread end and trim the tassel ends neatly.

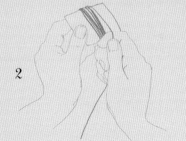

2

4

5

# Deep-Fringed Lampshade

Years of use leave lampshades yellowed and a bit tired-looking. Here we have revamped an old table lamp with some ultra-deep fringing. If this look is too over the top for your taste, buy fringing that is just the depth of the shade; alternatively, think about layering shorter fringing one above the other, working from the bottom of the shade up.

**MATERIALS**

Lampshade

Fringing

Tape measure

Scissors

Hot-glue gun

### INSTRUCTIONS

1. Measure the circumference of your lampshade and cut the fringing to length, adding an extra 5mm (¼in) for neatly finishing the ends.

2. Working a small area at a time, dab hot glue onto the rim of the shade and apply the fringing. Avoid large globs of glue, as these will seep through the fringing and leave unsightly visible marks.

3. When you have glued the fringing all the way around the lampshade, finish off by turning under the loose end and sticking it to the shade, making sure it slightly overlaps the starting point to give a neat finish.

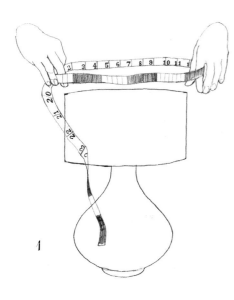

1

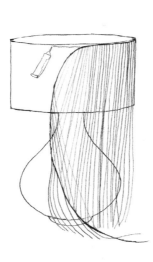

2

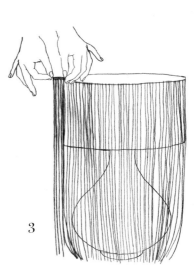

3

# Ribbon-Trimmed Pillowcases

You can trim pillowcases and sheets with ribbon so that they coordinate with the rest of your bedroom, or just to give them a splash of colour and charming detail. Choose ribbon that can stand up to machine-washing and check that the dye is colourfast: you don't want all your whites coming out a telltale pink-white or, worse still, a shade of grey.

## INSTRUCTIONS

1. Measure the width of the pillowcase from side seam to side seam and add an extra 3cm (1¼in) for the hems at both ends, then cut one length each of wide and narrow ribbon to this measurement.

2. Pin the wide ribbon to the top of the pillowcase, placing it about 1cm (½in) in from the open edge of the pillowcase and making sure it is straight. Turn under the hem allowance to make a neat edge at each of the side seams of the pillowcase, then tack the ribbon in place.

3. Machine-stitch the ribbon to the pillowcase, sewing along both edges of the ribbon using matching thread. Remove the tacking thread.

4. Pin the length of narrow ribbon centrally on top of the wide ribbon in the same way as before, tack in place, then machine-stitch. Remove the tacking thread and press the pillowcase lightly – making sure you don't burn the ribbon.

**MATERIALS**

Plain pillowcase

Ribbon, 5cm (2in) wide and 2cm (¾in) wide

Tape measure

Scissors

Pins

Needle

Tacking thread

Matching sewing thread

Sewing machine

Iron

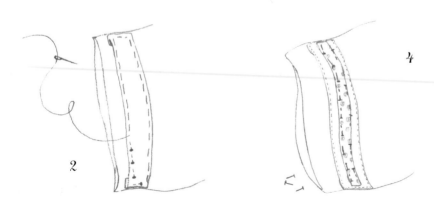

# Silk-Edged Top

Elevate a simple jersey top or skirt to something special by trimming it with ribbon. For this project the ribbon extends beyond the V-shaped neckline so that it can be tied in a pretty, ultra-feminine bow (see photograph overleaf). Experiment with velvet or satin ribbon, lace or even a sequin trim. On skirts, stitch ribbon around the hem or 10–15cm (4–6in) down from the waistband to add detail and a slightly 1950s feel.

### INSTRUCTIONS

1. Measure the length of ribbon you will need to trim the neckline, allowing sufficient length for the ties. Using an iron, press the ribbon in half widthways to create a sharp central crease along its length.

2. Fold the ribbon in half lengthways to find the middle, then pin it to the centre back of the top. The ribbon should sandwich the edge of the top, encasing it, with the pressed fold lying flush with the edge of the top. Pin it in place to secure it, then continue pinning the rest of the ribbon in place around the neckline of the top, working outwards from the centre on both sides.

3. When you reach the centre front of the top, continue pinning in half the loose ribbons on both sides (the bits that will tie the bow) and finish by turning the ends in on themselves to hide the raw edges.

4. Tack the ribbon in place, then machine-stitch using matching thread along the outside edge of the ribbon to secure in place. Remove the tacking thread.

### MATERIALS

Top

Silk ribbon, about 4cm (1¾in) wide

Tape measure

Iron

Pins

Needle

Tacking thread

Matching sewing thread

Sewing machine

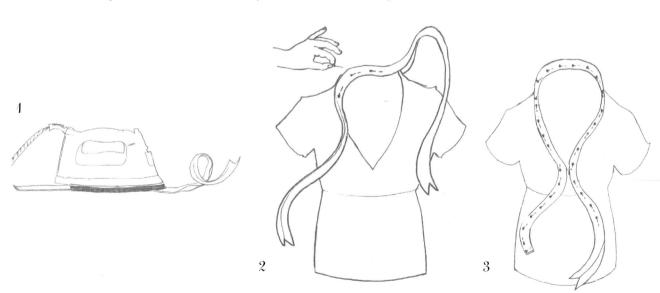

Patching

# Patch It Up

When I think of patches, I automatically picture the brown suede elbow patches on my grandpa's thick woolly cardigan, which according to my recollections he always seemed to wear. My other strong association with patches is from that period when it was fashionable to have ripped jeans and Liberty print fabric patched behind the holes. Thankfully the jeans are long gone, although you still can't beat an elbow patch for that true make-do-and-mend look.

Patching is much more interesting when it is used decoratively – instead of cutting out a boring old circle or square, experiment with a floral or star-shaped motif instead. After all, appliqué is really just a decorative form of patching, and once the raw edges of a hole have been turned under and tidied up you can cover it with some appliqué.

## Types of Patching

There are two different ways of patching: hand-patching and machine-patching. A hand patch is nearly always used to repair a hole. Traditionally it is done with fabric the same colour as the garment you are repairing, but I always think this looks a bit weird as it's obvious where the repair is, so why bother trying to hide it? If you are taking the time to mend something or extend its life, why not have some fun while you're at it and use a contrasting or patterned fabric that will add a new dimension. (For instructions on how to hand-patch, see the project on page 24.)

For the sewing- or time-challenged, you could always use an iron-on patch. These are pressed in place with a warm iron – the heat sticks the patch to the fabric you are mending. Choose from basic oval or rectangular patches or the large range of numbers, letters and motifs that are now available. But do think before ironing – what will it look like if you cover the seat of your trousers with a row of numbers? It may look good laid out flat, but the effect could be quite another thing when you put them on.

# How to Machine-Patch

Machine patching is much quicker than hand-patching, but somehow it never has quite the same charm. That said, it is good for upholstery and soft furnishings, as the stitching will hold for longer and stand up to harder wear.

1. Cut a square or rectangle 2–3cm (1–1½in) bigger than the worn area or hole, and tack in position on the right side of the fabric.

2. Using matching thread, machine zigzag stitch all round the edges to fix the patch.

3. Turn the fabric over and, using a pair of fine-pointed scissors, trim the worn areas to within 9mm (⅜in) of the stitched edge.

4. With the wrong side facing, machine zigzag stitch over the raw edges just trimmed.

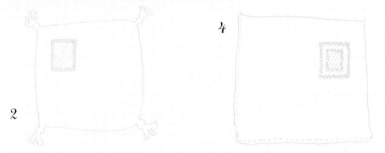

# Patching a Right-angle Tear

This is a good way of mending a tear or hole that is too large to be darned.

1. Bring the edges of the tear together by loosely oversewing them, working tiny stitches across the tear. Make sure that the stitches start and end at least 5mm (¼in) beyond each end of the tear.

2. On a tear on a worn garment or a pocket, first iron a square of iron-on interfacing to the wrong side before sewing the tear.

**TIP:** If you are trying to disguise a patch, make sure that the grain of the patch runs in the same direction as the grain of the fabric being repaired.

# Pretty Elbow Patch

No matter how many new clothes we buy, there is always one faithful item that we wear more than anything else. My weakness is woollen cardigans – warm and cosy in the winter; good to chuck on as the evening cools in early summer. Aside from pilling, woollen clothing tends to wear quickest at the elbows, a problem that can be swiftly fixed with a couple of simple patches. While this project uses a pretty contrasting floral fabric, you can just as easily make more subtle patches using matching or plain fabric.

**MATERIALS**

Cardigan or jumper

Fabric for patch

Scissors

Tape measure

Pins

Needle

Tacking thread

Matching sewing thread

### INSTRUCTIONS

1. Cut a patch 3–4cm (1¼–1¾in) larger than the worn area. For the elbow, an oval shape is best as this fits and moves better than a square or rectangular patch. Pin the patch over the worn area on the right side of the fabric.

2. Tack 5mm (¼in) in from the raw edge with running stitch to secure the patch loosely in place, and cut notches out of the curves so that the patch will lie flat.

3. Turn under the raw edges and pin, then tack to hold them in place.

4. Using small hemming stitches, sew the patch to the fabric with matching thread. Remove the inner row of tacking stitch.

5. On the wrong side, trim away the worn fabric up to 5mm (¼in) away from the stitched edge of the patch – take care not to cut the patch.

6. Using buttonhole stitch, secure the raw edges of the fabric, being careful not to stitch into the front side of the patch. Finally, remove the tacking stitches.

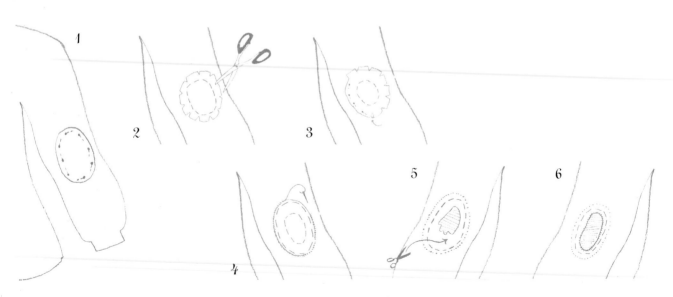

# Floral Jeans Patch

Repair and hide a ripped pocket with a decorative patch. A bit more advanced than a simple fabric patch, this embroidered flower motif can be simplified if you're not confident on the sewing machine. Pick out the petal shapes with hand embroidery or, even simpler, use a fabric pen instead.

## INSTRUCTIONS

1. Using a suitable pen, trace the outline of the flower motif on page 90 onto the dissolvable transparent fabric to create a template.

2. Pin the design to the patch fabric, then secure the fabric in an embroidery hoop to keep it taut while stitching.

3. Using a darning foot, drop the fabric feeder feet in the plate of your sewing machine so that you can move the fabric around easily when sewing. Select zigzag stitch; make sure the stitch length is at 0 so that each stitch is placed next to the other with no gap in between, allowing you to make a solid line. (Practise on a scrap of fabric first.) Trace the petal outlines with the sewing machine to fill in the flower detail.

4. Remove the embroidery hoop and, following the manufacturer's instructions, place the embroidered fabric in water to dissolve the template, then iron dry on the reverse.

5. Following the manufacturer's instructions, apply iron-on adhesive web to the wrong side of the fabric.

6. Taking care not to snip any stitches, cut out the flower motif.

7. Using an iron and following the iron-on adhesive web manufacturer's instructions, secure the motif to your jeans, making sure you cover the tear.

## MATERIALS

Jeans

Pen

Fabric for patch

Dissolvable transparent fabric

Embroidery hoop

Iron-on adhesive web

Sewing machine

Sewing thread

Iron

Scissors

**TIP:** Reinforce the tear further by first applying an iron-on patch to the inside of the pocket before adding the embroidered patch to the outside of the pocket.

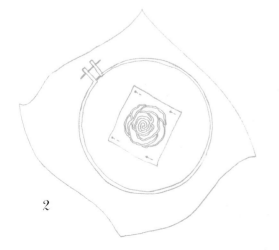

2

3

6

# Patchwork Footstool

This old stool came from a junk shop and its horsehair stuffing was in good nick, but the cover was torn. Leftover strips of tweed fabric have been patched together to make the new cover. You can scale this project up to create chair and seat-pad covers; if you have plenty of time, you could experiment with piecing together more complex geometric patterns such as hexagons.

**INSTRUCTIONS**

1. Measure the width and length of your footstool, and cut enough strips of fabric to fit, adding a 2cm (1in) seam allowance to each strip.

2. Pin together all the strips of fabric (right sides together) to make a single rectangle, then tack to hold in place.

3. Stitch the seams and press flat using an iron and damp tea towel or pressing cloth (which should be placed on top of the seam). Remove the tacking thread.

4. Position the fabric on the stool and, using a few pins, attach it to the stool.

5. Turn the stool upside down. Starting on one of the longest sides and working from the middle outwards, turn the raw edge of the fabric under and use a staple gun to staple the fabric to the underside of the stool.

6. Remove any holding pins and repeat the previous step on the opposite long side of the stool, pulling the fabric taut and turning it under to make a neat edge.

7. Repeat for the two remaining sides of the stool, folding the fabric neatly in on itself at the corners.

**TIP:** Depending on the design of your stool, the staples may be visible. If so, cover them by gluing a length of matching binding or trimming around the edges. (See pages 10–11 for inspiration.)

**MATERIALS**

Footstool

Tape measure

Tweed or other fabric

Scissors

Pins

Needle

Tacking thread

Matching sewing thread

Sewing machine

Iron

Tea towel or pressing cloth

Staple gun

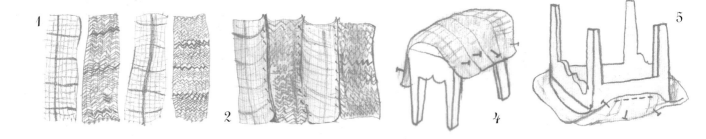

Hemming

# Hemmed In

Apart from tidying up raw edges, hems add weight to clothes or curtains and drapes, helping them to hang properly. It's also usually the last job to be done when you are sewing, and the fabric and style of the item often determine the kind of hem you should use. The best hems are those sewn by hand, as from the right side of the fabric they are practically invisible. Never rush — always take your time and make sure the hem is perfectly level. When hemming trousers, both legs must be the same length — obvious I know, but you'd be surprised. And use seam binding to neaten and protect the edges of any fabric that frays easily.

## Types of Hem

The depth of a hem depends entirely on what the item is; curtains and drapes have very deep hems, while stretchy fashion fabrics can have as little as 3mm (⅛in). For a really professional finish, use a floor-standing hem ruler to measure your hem and mark the hemline with pins at the same height all the way round.

**MACHINE-STITCHED HEMS** are visible from the right side of the fabric. This type of hem should be used on knitted fabrics and where topstitching is a feature rather than an eyesore. Always press the hemline in place on the wrong side before stitching — this will help keep it even.

**EDGE-STITCHED HEMS** are good for light- and medium-weight fabrics. They need to be pressed from the wrong side, otherwise a ridge will form on the right side. Turn under 5mm (¼in) along the raw edge and machine-stitch close to the fold to leave a neat edge. Turn up the hem and slipstitch in place.

**ZIGZAG HEMS** are good for stretchy fabrics and fabrics that fray easily. Start by neatening the edge with machine zigzag stitch. Turn up the hem and press, pin, then tack. Slipstitch in place and remove the tacking. Zigzag hems lie very flat.

**DOUBLE HEMS** are used mostly on transparent fabrics such as voile, chiffon or organza, and for sheer curtains. First decide on the finished hem length, then mark with pins and tack so that you have a line to follow. Then decide how deep your hem will be. If it is 4cm (1¾in), double this figure (8cm/3½in) and measure down from the marked hemline. Cut the fabric to this length. Fold the hem in half (4cm) so that the raw edge lies along the hemline. Fold up the hem again (4cm), then pin and tack in place. Machine- or slipstitch the hem, then remove the tacking.

**NARROW HEMS** are most often used for clothing made from lightweight fabrics such as shirts. The edge can be machine-stitched or slipstitched. Turn under 5mm (¼in) along the raw edge, then turn up a narrow hem. Slipstitch in place.

**HAND-ROLLED HEMS** have a soft and subtle finish that makes them good for use with silk and sheer fabrics. You will often find them used to finish the edges of silk scarves. It takes quite a while to do because the fabric has to be rolled between your finger and thumb, then slipstitched. Machine-stitch 5mm (¼in) in from the hemline and trim the fabric close to the stitching. Roll the edge, enclosing the machine stitching, then slipstitch to hold in place, making sure you catch only a single thread of the fabric so that the stitches are almost invisible.

**MACHINE-ROLLED HEMS** have a much stiffer finish than hand-rolled hems, because they have two rows of stitching. These are good for fine fabrics such as cotton lawn that need a very neat finish. Turn under 5mm (¼in) and machine-stitch along the fold to give a neat edge. Then turn under another 5mm (¼in) and machine-stitch through both layers of the hem to secure in place.

# Five Steps to a Perfect Hem

No matter what item you're sewing, follow these steps for a successful finish.

1. Use pins to mark your hemline, then tack along this line in a contrasting thread.

2. Measure the depth of hem needed, allowing for turnings or seam allowances, and mark this line with pins. Trim the fabric to the correct length.

3. Trim any side seam allowances that fall below the tacked hemline to 5mm (¼in). This helps the finished hem to lie flat.

4. Machine-stitch the raw edge with zigzag stitch. Turn up the hem halfway and then fold it over again so that the tacked hemline becomes the bottom edge of the garment or item you are sewing; pin and then tack to hold the hem in place.

5. Carefully ease any fullness in the hem so that it lies evenly and flat, then slipstitch.

2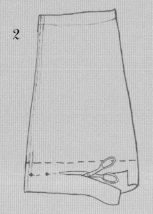

3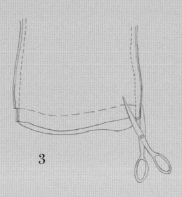

4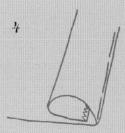

# Reinspired Curtains

Don't throw out your curtains or drapes when you move house; if they are too short, recycle them by adding panels of fabric to lengthen them. This project works well on plain curtains – you can add a toning panel of patterned fabric to tie in with your new colour scheme.

### INSTRUCTIONS

1. Work out the depth of fabric required to lengthen your curtains, and add a 3cm (1¼in) hem allowance to this measurement. Measure the width of the curtain, and add a 10cm (4in) hem allowance to this measurement. Cut the fabric panel and finish the raw edges with zigzag stitch.

2. Decide where you want the top edge of your curtain panel to start, and cut a straight line along the width of the curtain. Finish the raw edges using zigzag stitch.

3. With right sides together, pin the top edge of the curtain panel and the top half of the curtain together, allowing a 1.5cm (⅝in) seam; tack, then machine-stitch. Remove the tacking thread, then press the seam open using the steam setting on your iron.

4. Repeat this process to attach the base of the panel to the bottom half of the curtain.

5. Finish the side edges by turning in the fabric and slipstitching or machine-stitching in place.

**TIP:** If your curtains are lined, you will need to remove the lining completely before adding the panel, and replace it after you have lengthened the curtains. (You will obviously also need to lengthen the lining.)

### MATERIALS

Curtains or drapes

Fabric

Tape measure

Scissors

Matching sewing thread

Sewing machine

Pins

Needle

Tacking thread

Iron

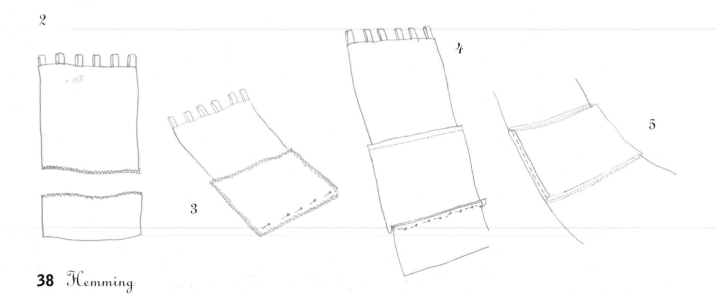

# Tier-Hemmed Skirt

You can lengthen and dress up a simple skirt by adding a false hem such as this lace-and-ribbon one. This technique can also be used on trouser legs or cuffs. Choose fabrics in a toning colour that are the same weight as your skirt; if you wish, you can also try gathering the hem before attaching it for a ruffled effect.

### INSTRUCTIONS

1. Measure the circumference of your hem, adding a 2cm (1¾in) seam allowance. Work out how long you want the hem to be, add 2cm (1in) hem allowance to this measurement as well, and cut the lace fabric to length.

2. Finish the top and bottom raw edges of the lace false hem with zigzag stitch. Turn up a 1cm (½in) hem allowance along the bottom edge of the fabric and pin, then machine-stitch in place, and press flat.

3. If you wish to add ribbon trim, as here, pin the ribbon to the right side of the bottom edge of the false hem; tack, then stitch in place.

4. Turn the skirt inside out and pin the false hem to the skirt, 3cm (1¼in) above the hem of the skirt to create a tier. Tack, then machine-stitch in place.

5. Turn the skirt right way out and pin another row of ribbon trim along the edge of the skirt hem. Tack in place and topstitch the ribbon along the top and bottom edges for a neat finish. Remove all the tacking thread.

**TIP:** If you don't want a tier effect, in step 4 join the false hem to the hem of the skirt, rather than attaching it 3cm (1¼in) above. Then, when you topstitch the ribbon trim in step 5, you will secure both the ribbon and false hem in place.

### MATERIALS

Skirt

Tape measure

Lace

Scissors

Pins

Matching sewing thread

Sewing machine

Tacking thread

Needle

Iron

Ribbon (optional)

Needle

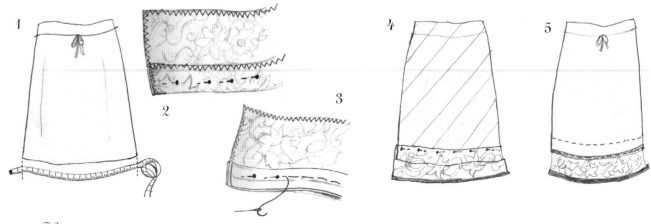

# Lace-Topped Sheets

Transform a simple sheet into something far more special with a lace-edged hem. You can use this type of hemming to lengthen a sheet – if it's not already long enough – so that you can fold the top part over an eiderdown or quilt to make a deep and pretty border on display just below the pillows (see photograph overleaf). Hemming the sheet provides a more substantial and heavier edge, which emphasizes the lace trim.

**MATERIALS**

Sheet

Matching fabric, the width of the sheet and 15cm (6in) deep (deeper if you need to add length to the sheet)

Scissors

Tape measure

Iron

Pins

Needle

Tacking thread

Matching sewing thread

Sewing machine

Lace trim measuring the width of the sheet

## INSTRUCTIONS

1. Cut a piece of the fabric that matches your sheet 15cm (6in) deep and the same width as your sheet, plus a 1.5cm (⅝in) seam allowance on both sides. Using a zigzag stitch, finish the raw edges. Press under a 1.5cm (⅝in) hem allowance along the top and bottom edges. Fold the fabric in half, so that the top and bottom edges meet with the wrong sides together, and press.

2. Pin one edge of fabric to the top edge of the sheet, with wrong sides together, and tack, then machine-stitch in place, and remove the tacking thread. Turn in the seam allowance on both sides of the panel section and press to create neat edges.

3. Take the unattached edge of the panel section and fold it over the top edge of the sheet, sandwiching the top edge of the sheet. Make sure the seam allowance is turned under, then pin it to the other side of the sheet to make a hem and tack in place. Topstitch using the sewing machine, then remove the tacking thread and press the hem to create a flat seam.

4. Close the sides of the hem on both sides using slipstitch.

5. Pin the lace to the top edge of the hemmed sheet and either hand-stitch in place or tack then machine-stitch the lace to the sheet.

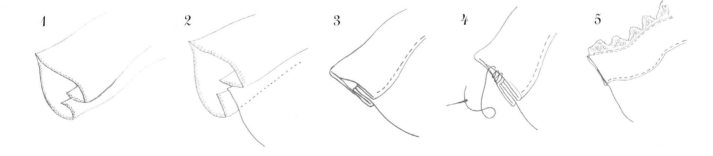

# Darning & Disguising

# Darn Good Darning

Darning is definitely one of those make-do-and-mend skills that have fallen by the wayside. But you can bet that your grandmother was a true expert at it, with socks, sweaters, gloves and the knees in your grandfather's gardening trousers all given a life extension with a bit of nifty darning.

This technique is used for repairing small holes or tears, and to reinforce worn fabric before it ends up in holes. Darning is one of those 'mend it' techniques that can seem a little daunting, but think of it as simply weaving on a small scale using a needle, and you've got it covered.

No matter how neatly you darn an area, on close inspection you will still be able to spot it. Still, while your best cashmere sweater that you accidentally snagged on a hook as you rushed out of the door to get to work on time might not be smart enough for the office any more, with a spot of darning it'll still be good enough to wear while lazing around at home.

## Darning by Hand

1. Start with a long length of thread. Tack a circle or square of small running stitches around the outside edge of the hole or worn area.

2. Work parallel rows of small running stitches backwards and forwards across the fabric within the area you have tacked. Make sure you leave a small loop at the end of each row so that the thread doesn't pull too tightly. In the area where the hole or worn patch is, stitch long threads in parallel rows across it, and continue with running stitches on the fabric on each side.

3. Turn the fabric around so that the threads you have just stitched lie vertically. Using the same thread, weave over and under the stitches and fabric thread, covering the whole area but working rows at right angles to the previous rows. Again, avoid pulling the threads too tightly.

**WHAT YOU NEED**

Always choose a thread that matches the colour of your fabric as closely as possible – unless, of course, you wish to make a feature of your darning patch.

Use a thread that is slightly thinner than the threads of the fabric you are mending, so that your darning doesn't get too chunky.

You can use an ordinary needle, but a darning needle is good for use on bigger holes – these are quite long and have a large eye.

If you plan to become a darning diva, it's worth buying a darning 'egg' or 'mushroom'. These are made of either plastic or wood, and have a rounded shape across which you support your fabric while you are darning. Keep your eyes peeled at flea markets, where you can often pick up an old wooden darning mushroom.

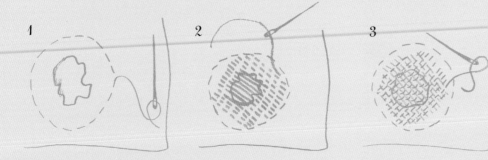

# Darning by Machine

Machine-darning gives a less subtle effect than darning by hand and is best kept for reinforcing worn fabric, rather than repairing a hole. Machine-stitching is denser than hand-stitching, so the darned area can end up a bit on the stiff side.

1. Fit your machine with the darning foot, and set the machine for straight stitch with the stitch length at zero.

2. Tack a circle or square of running stitches around the outside of the worn area. If you can, stretch the fabric into an embroidery hoop, as this will make it easier to manoeuvre and keep the fabric flat on the needle plate.

3. Lower the darning foot into place and stitch parallel rows closely together, working backwards and forwards across the tacked area.

4. When you have completed your circle or square, stop with the needle still in the fabric and turn the hoop 90° so that the stitches now run the other way.

5. Again, stitch parallel rows, but make them slightly further apart than before, and continue to fill the whole area with a stitched grid.

6. If you are using this method to fill a hole, you will need to turn the fabric and stitch another set of parallel rows across the entire area.

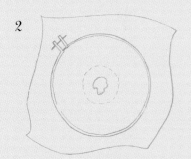
2

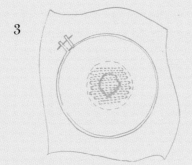
3

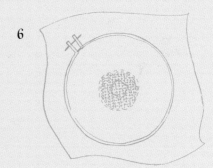
6

# Silk Corsages

Silk corsages are relatively quick to make, so you can easily make one to match every outfit. They are also a great way of disguising a patch of not-so-invisible darning. For this corsage I have used two different weights of silk and decorated the centre with gold and shell-coloured buttons, but you could just as easily make them with cute cotton florals and beaded centres.

**MATERIALS**

2 different lengths of silk fabric or netting

Tape measure

Scissors

Iron

Matchng sewing thread

Sewing machine

Needle

Fabric glue

Selection of buttons

Iron-on interfacing

Badge pin

**INSTRUCTIONS**

1. First cut a rectangular piece of fabric for the outer ruffle. It should measure roughly 10cm x 45cm (4in x 18in). Cut a smaller piece from the second fabric for the inner ruffle, measuring 5cm x 30cm (2in x 12in). Taking the first piece of fabric, press it in half along the length with wrong sides together; repeat for the second piece of fabric.

2. Lay the largest fabric strip out flat and, with right sides together, stitch the short ends together on the sewing machine, allowing a 1cm (½in) seam allowance, to create a circle of fabric.

3. Fold the fabric back in half along the pressed top edge so that wrong sides are together and, using running stitch, stitch along the bottom edge of the fabric ring, 5mm (¼in) in from the edge.

4. When you have gone full circle, carefully pull the thread tight so that the fabric ruffles up to create a tight circle, and secure the thread with a double knot. Repeat steps 2–4 for the other piece of fabric.

5. Using fabric glue, attach the smaller ruffle centrally on top of the larger ruffle. Sew buttons to the centre of the corsage, using them to disguise any raw edges.

6. Iron a patch of matching fabric onto iron-on interfacing. Cut a circle from this fabric measuring 2–3cm (¾–1¼in) in diameter (or big enough to cover the raw edge on the back of the corsage), and use fabric glue to attach this to the centre of the back of the corsage. Finally, add a safety pin or badge pin.

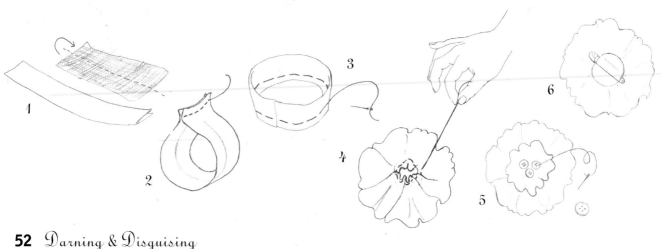

# Floral Appliqué

This technique is as old as the hills and is a great way of adding decoration and disguising a ripped hem in a skirt. You don't have to use a floral motif; simple geometric blocks can work equally well. Consider the fabric you use carefully; it needs to be the same or a lighter weight than the clothing you are attaching it to, so that it doesn't alter the way it hangs (see photograph overleaf). Appliqué can be done by machine or hand.

## INSTRUCTIONS

1. First design a motif, or trace the template given on page 90. Alternatively, cut out actual flower shapes from a floral printed fabric and use these as your motif.

2. Iron the motif or fabric onto interfacing to make it easier to work with and to add strength to intricate shapes.

3. Add detail to the design by using freehand running stitch on your machine to give outlines around the edges of your motif. Don't worry if they are wobbly or a bit messy – this will enhance the design.

4. Decorate the centre of the floral motifs with sequins and beads. Push the needle and thread through the centre of the motif from back to front. Thread a sequin onto the needle, then a bead, then push the needle back through the sequin's centre and secure with a knot on the reverse.

5. Using a pair of sharp, fine scissors, cut out all your motifs and arrange them on the skirt – covering any damaged areas you are trying to disguise – so that they form a pleasing pattern. When you are happy with their position, pin them in place.

6. Using matching thread, neatly slipstitch the motifs to the skirt.

**MATERIALS**

Fabric (satin and silk chiffon are good choices)

Tracing paper

Scissors

Iron

Iron-on interfacing

Sewing machine

Matching sewing thread

Sequins and beads

Needle

**TIP** If you are using a fabric that frays easily, you will need to machine zigzag stitch around edges after step 2, unless you would like a frayed look as part of the design, as shown here.

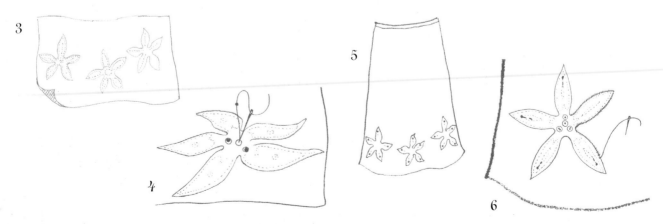

3

4

5

6

# Vintage Lace Cardigan

It's quite easy to pick up beautiful fragments of old lace from antiques stores and textiles fairs. For this project I have used a half-doily to disguise a darned patch in the back of a cardigan. The old lace collar was added for extra decoration and because it had been sitting in the cupboard for a long time waiting to be used (see photograph overleaf).

## INSTRUCTIONS

1. Darn any holes in your cardigan or jumper using the techniques described at the start of this chapter on pages 50–1.

2. Lay the cardigan out flat, and play around with the positioning of your lace panels. When you feel they are in the right place, pin them to the cardigan.

3. Using a fine needle and thread, slipstitch around the edges of the lace to secure it to the cardigan, then remove the pins.

**TIP:** To whiten discoloured lace panels and doilies, try soaking them in a solution of diluted hydrogen peroxide, which is available from chemists. Do not use ordinary bleach (chlorine), as it is too harsh.

**MATERIALS**

Cardigan or jumper

Darning 'egg' or 'mushroom'

Darning needle

Matching darning thread

Scissors

Vintage lace collars and/or doilies

Pins

Needle

Matching sewing thread

2

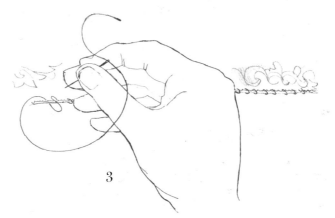
3

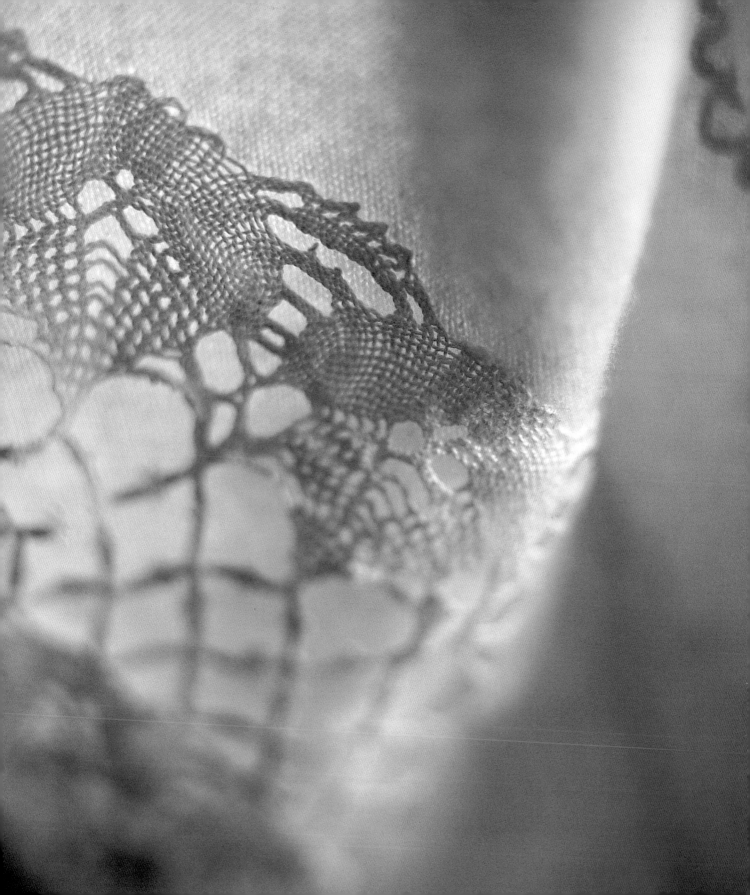

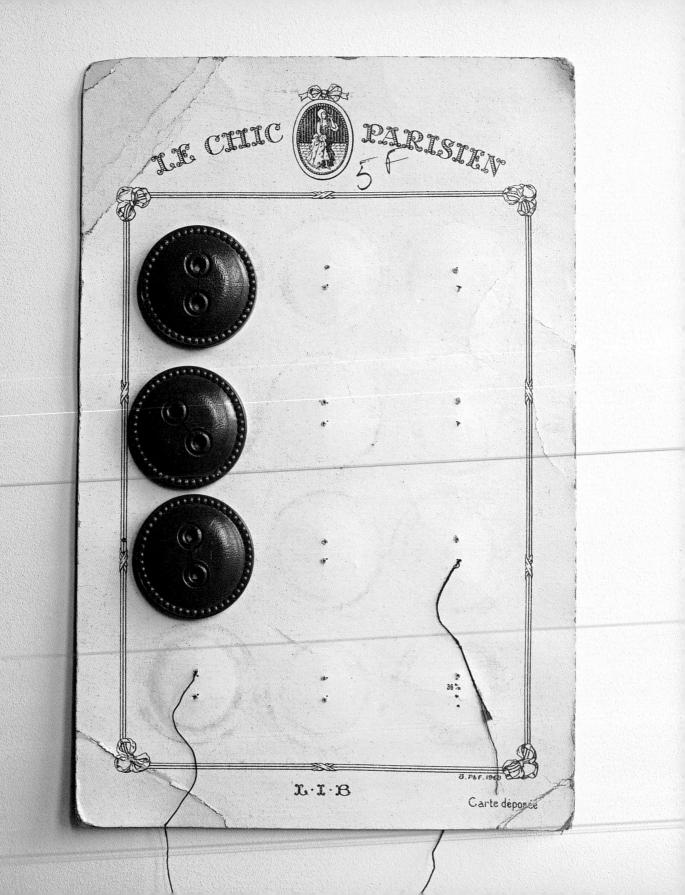

# Customizing

# Custom-Made

Customizing has to be my favourite aspect of the whole make-do-and-mend vibe. It's the fun part – adding a little bit of something or even taking away something that's already there to revamp an item that's been knocking around the house for a while. The whole point of customizing is to make your mark, to take what might be quite an ordinary object and personalize it. It's also a great way of making gifts that have that home-made feel for friends and family, without you needing to be a stitching guru or having to start from scratch.

## Five Ideas for Customizing Cushions

1. Cut squares out of old tea towels and stitch them onto plain cushions; decorate the edges with a row of cross-stitch for homespun country style.

2. Splash out on some suede fringing, and neatly stitch it around the edge of a square or round cushion cover.

3. Decorate a cushion with an old silk scarf. To make it a little more unusual, sew the scarf onto a piece of backing fabric first and, using freehand stitching on your sewing machine, trace outlines of the design in coloured thread. You could then cut away the background of the scarf to show just the design and to reveal the backing fabric.

4. Use old fabric badges or military brass buttons to decorate the front of a cushion cover. Sew them randomly onto patches of coloured fabric, or cover the entire cushion with them.

5. For children's rooms, create fun cushion covers by ironing on series of numbers or spell out their names in outsized letters. Most haberdashery shops sell heat-adhesive number and letter patches.

## Five Ideas for Customizing Clothing

1. Thread silk ribbon around the waist of a mohair jumper, to add feminine detail – use two rows of ribbon so that it makes more of a statement, and tie them in a bow at the ends.

2. Change the buttons on coats – choose something bold and decorative to dress up a plain black coat. Alternatively, think about adding rows of small buttons to the wrists of a jumper or cardigan for a tailored 1950s look.

**CUSTOMIZING KIT**

When you are out and about, keep a look out for bits and pieces on sale that you can stash away and use next time you are indulging in a spot of customizing.

Sequins in different colours and sizes – for that instant disco glam.

Buttons – look for unusual shapes and colours, or natural materials such as wood, horn and shell. Junk or vintage stores often stock old sheets of them.

Ribbon and braid – ideal for using on clothing and soft furnishings to add decorative detail.

Decorative fabric panels – embroidered handkerchiefs and silk panels are great for stitching onto a plain-coloured bag to make it more individual. Or keep an eye out for offcuts of large floral-patterned fabrics, and cut out a single bloom to use for appliqué.

Feathers and fringing – these are fantastic for a heady and decadent look or for fancy dress!

3. Sequins add instant glamour – scatter a scarf with sequins, gluing them in place with fabric glue. For more sequin ideas, see the project on page 72.

4. Trim the neck and sleeve edges of T-shirts with contrasting coloured ribbon to dress them up. You could also do this to strengthen the buttonholes on a wool cardigan, but you will need to cut holes for the buttons to pass through, and finish the raw edges with buttonhole stitch.

5. Decorate the edge of a bag or skirt by stitching on tiny velvet or silk flower petals. Stitch them so that they overlap, or spread them out and dot them about randomly for a less ordered appearance.

# Five Ideas for Customizing around the Home

1. Use a hot-glue gun to attach ribbon to the top and bottom edges of a lampshade for an instant lift.

2. Trim 5cm (2in) in from the edge of an Oxford pillowcase with rickrack ribbon to create a border. Make sure you choose cotton rickrack so that the finished pillowcase can still be machine-washed.

3. Use a stencil and fabric paint to add monograms to table linen or bed sheets. To make the results more decorative, you could also sew a row of backstitch around the edge of the monogram.

4. Decorate the lower edge of a Roman blind with beaded fringing that catches the light when the blind is pulled up during the day.

5. Plasticized fabrics make great practical tablecloths: choose a plain colour, then cut it to give it a zigzag or scallop-shaped edge. Add extra decoration by using a leather punch to make holes all along the shaped edge – this gives a lacy effect to the finished tablecloth.

# Ribbon-Threaded Blanket

This is probably the quickest and simplest project in the book. Here we have threaded ribbon through a loosely woven mohair throw; you could do the same with any loosely woven blanket. For a similar effect on a sheet or travel rug, try using embroidery thread or wool with a running stitch.

**MATERIALS**

Mohair or other suitable loose-weave blanket

Velvet ribbon

Tape measure

Scissors

Tapestry needle with large eye

Needle

Matching sewing thread

**INSTRUCTIONS**

1. Cut two pieces of ribbon 20cm (8in) longer than the width of the blanket. Thread the tapestry needle with the first ribbon and pull through from wrong to right side, leaving 1cm (½in) loose on the reverse. Secure the end of the ribbon on the underside of the blanket, turning the raw end under and slipstitching it in place.

2. With even stitches, weave the ribbon in and out along the bottom edge of the blanket, making sure the ribbon doesn't twist and lies flat. Use the bottom of the blanket as a guide to keep your line of stitching straight.

3. When you reach the end, leave at least 10cm (4in) of loose ribbon.

4. Return to the starting point and repeat for the second row of ribbon, placing it about 1cm (½in) above the first row and keeping the lines parallel.

5. Tie the loose ribbon ends into a bow to secure.

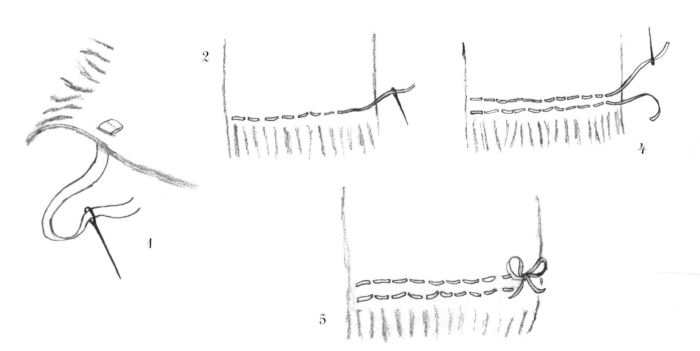

# Buckle & Ribbon Cushion

Create a boudoir effect or add a spot of glamour to a beaten-up leather sofa by decorating a plain cushion cover with silk ribbon and sparkly buckles. As an alternative to buckles, you could stitch shell buttons onto the lengths of ribbon instead, for an equally decorative effect.

## INSTRUCTIONS

1. Cut however many pieces of ribbon you want to the length of the cushion, adding 2cm (1in) seam allowance.

2. Position the ribbons roughly on the cushion front in your chosen design. On this cushion there is a wide turquoise ribbon parallel to a narrow black velvet ribbon on one side and, at right angles to them, another wide turquoise ribbon with a pink ribbon placed centrally on top of it (see photograph overleaf). Thread the buckles onto the ribbons.

3. When you are happy with the design, make sure the ribbons are straight and the raw ends are turned under, then pin and tack in place.

4. Using matching thread, sew the ribbons to the cushion cover, machine-stitching along both edges of the ribbons and stitching right up to the edges of the buckles, as close as you can. Remove the tacking thread.

**TIP:** You can use this technique to decorate a blanket or even loose covers on a chair – but position the buckles on the back or sides so that it is comfortable to sit in. Alternatively, you could decorate a bag or the waistband of a skirt or trousers.

### MATERIALS

Plain cushion cover

Silk ribbon

Tape measure

Scissors

Diamanté buckles or brooches

Pins

Needle

Tacking thread

Matching sewing thread

Sewing machine

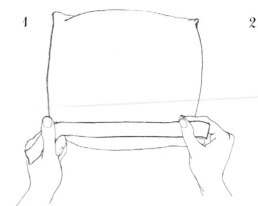

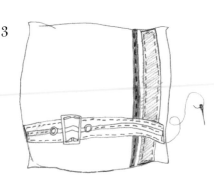

# Sequinned Top

Sewing on sequins by hand can take for ever, but as long as you are not too ambitious and in the right frame of mind it can be very effective. For this project we took a simple jersey top and added a butterfly motif, sequin-edged ties and a scattered-sequin panel to give it a bit more va va voom (see photograph overleaf).

### INSTRUCTIONS

1. Using tracing paper, trace the butterfly motif on page 91, then transfer the design onto card and cut out the template.

2. Position and pin the template in place on the jersey top and, using a fabric pen, trace around the edge of the template with a dotted line. Add in two dotted lines for antennae. Remove the template, and add a dotted line centrally between the wings for the butterfly's body.

3. Attach sequins by pushing the needle and thread through the top from back to front, threading on a sequin, then pushing the needle back through the top just in front of the sequin. Bring the needle back up through the top where the centre of the next sequin should be, then thread on the next sequin. Make sure you use a matching thread, as it will be visible. Continue around the edge of the butterfly until complete, then attach small sequins or beads for the antennae in the same way.

4. To sew a line of overlapping sequins (as we have along the edge of the ties and front panel of this top), work from right to left. Push the needle and thread up through the fabric and thread a sequin onto the needle, make a stitch over the left side of the sequin and take the needle back through the top. Bring the needle back through to the front of the top so that it is half the width of a sequin away from the attached sequin; thread the next sequin onto the needle and repeat.

5. The panel of random sequins at the bottom of the top is created by using the same technique as in step 3. Try to avoid forming obvious 'lines' of sequins when sewing this section, keeping their placement as random as possible.

MATERIALS

Jersey top

Sequins

Small sequins or beads

Needle

Matching sewing thread

Tracing paper

Card

Scissors

Pins

Fabric pen

**TIP:** When washing a sequinned top, do it carefully by hand, using tepid water and soap flakes. Do not wring or spin dry.

*Reinventing*

# Reinvention at Heart

Reinventing is at the heart of making do. If an item of clothing is beyond repair and wear, consider what else it might be used for before discarding it. Can you use the sequins on a once-glamorous skirt to decorate your Christmas cards or add some sparkle to the neckline of a top? Can a panel of decorative embroidery on an out-of-date evening dress be patched onto the front of a cushion cover to transform it into something special?

Reusing elements of clothing in this manner is a way of keeping things you love around you. The same applies with many household items. For instance, large curtains or drapes that have faded at the edges from exposure to the sun can be cut down to fit smaller windows. Don't buy a new chair or sofa simply because the fabric has worn; learn to make loose covers or reupholster it. These kinds of projects can seem daunting but, if you take your time and do them bit by bit, they're really not as difficult as you might think. If you want a professional finish, it's worth remembering that although having furniture re-covered might seem expensive, it's usually cheaper than buying new pieces.

## Five Ideas for Cushions

1. Don't throw away old linen sheets that have worn thin – cut them up into as many good pieces of cloth as you can, then make them into lavender sachets or cushion covers and embroider them with a monogram.

2. Boil-wash old wool jumpers, then cut them up to make cuddly patchwork cushions or even a small baby blanket. Tidy the raw edges by binding with a length of ribbon. Alternatively, use the felted fabric to make a hot-water bottle cover. (For more details on boil-washing, see the pompom cushion instructions on page 86.)

3. Cut the legs off old jeans and fill with a bolster cushion, tie the ends with cotton braid and use them to decorate a bed dressed with blue-and-white gingham linen. For a smarter, more tailored look, the legs of tweed or herringbone-patterned trousers neatly finished at the ends with velvet drawstring ties can be used on a cushion to adorn a bed or sofa.

4. Cut up torn or stained blankets and make them into beanbag floor cushions, stitching the edging with contrasting blanket stitch.

5. Weave lengths of leftover ribbon together to create a panel, which you can then back with fabric and make them into a cushion cover or tablemats.

# Five More Reinventing Ideas

1. An old silk skirt or shirt can be cut up and strips sewn into lengths of drawn ruffles that you can then use to edge another skirt, a tablecloth, a sheet, or even curtains or drapes. To make the ruffles, sew a line of running stitch down the centre of the strip of fabric, secure the thread at one end, then pull the loose end to make the ruffle. Tie the end, then machine-stitch a row of running stitch down the centre and unpick the hand-sewn running stitch.

2. Denim jackets and jeans can be patched together to create fun and durable covers for stools or chairs. Rather than trying to conceal the stitches, make them part of the design using coloured thread and decorative stitches such as blanket stitch and backstitch.

3. Old lace doilies, which are often found in junk shops, look pretty stitched onto a length of muslin to create a curtain or drape. Alternatively, use them as a feminine backdrop for old black-and-white photographs: place the lace in a large frame so that you can see the entire decorative border, then simply position the photograph in the centre, attaching it with double-sided photo-mounting tape.

4. Scraps of coloured fabric, such as felt or fabric with small floral patterns, look great when cut into small flower-shaped motifs. Layer them so that the petals overlap and, with the largest petals at the bottom, join them together using a few decorative stitches that look like a stamen, then use to decorate a plain lampshade or stick them onto stiff paper to make gift cards.

5. Use a necktie to make a strap for a fabric bag. Alternatively, plait together three silk scarves and use as a handle.

# Fabric Clutch Bag

This project uses an out-of-fashion but much-loved skirt as its foundation. The inner bag and lining is made from the lining of the skirt, and the addition of a ruffled edge helps to make it a little dressier. You don't have to use an old skirt — any fabric that you have held onto can be used. Think about embellishing the bag further with sequins and beads once you've made it (see photograph overleaf).

### INSTRUCTIONS

1. Cut out two panels of lining fabric measuring 18 x 28cm (7 x 11 in) and one lace panel also measuring 18 x 28cm (7 x 11in). Cut out four triangular gusset pieces of lining material measuring 8 x 8 x 11cm (3½ x 3½ x 4½in).

2. Press the two pieces of lining fabric in half lengthwise. Take one piece of lining fabric and two gusset pieces, and pin the edges of one gusset piece to one end of the folded lining fabric, allowing a 1cm (½in) seam. Repeat for the other gusset so that you are left with a bag shape. Tack and machine-stitch, then remove the tacking thread.

3. Repeat for the other piece of lining fabric. Then, with right sides together, place one piece of lining fabric inside the other.

4. Tack all the top edges together, leaving a gap in the middle of one of the long edges so that you can turn the bag right side out. Stitch together, remembering to leave a gap, then remove the tacking.

5. Trim and press the seams, then turn the lining fabric right sides out. Turn under the raw edges of the gap and slipstitch to close.

6. Pin the lace panel to the outer side of the bag, then tack in place. Sew the lace to the lining fabric using slipstitch and keeping the stitches as close to the edge of the lace as possible. Remove the tacking.

7. Now attach clasp to the bag. It is advisable to mask the clasp and edges of the bag with masking tape to protect them from glue. Open the clasp and squeeze glue into the groove on all three sides of one half of the clasp.

8. Using a tapestry needle, push the edges of the bag into place, making sure they are pushed right in so that the bag fits the clasp tightly. Leave until completely dry, then repeat for the other side of the bag. When the glue is completely dry, carefully remove the masking tape. Then, using matching embroidery thread, reinforce by oversewing the edges of the bag and clasp.

9. To make the ruffle for the front of the bag, cut a length of lace 30cm (12in) long and 10cm (4in) deep. Turn under the raw top edge, allowing a 1cm (½in) hem, and stitch. By hand, sew along the top edge of the ruffle using running stitch. Pull the thread to scrunch up the ruffle and pin it in position on the front of the bag. Sew it in place using slipstitch. Add a few sequins or beads, using the technique in step 3 on page 72.

## MATERIALS

Old lace skirt and lining

Tape measure

Scissors

Iron

Pins

Needle

Tacking thread

Matching sewing thread

Sewing machine

17cm (6½in) purse/bag clasp (grooved on all three sides to allow you to push the fabric in)

Strong fabric glue

Masking tape

Tapestry needle

Matching embroidery thread

Sequins or beads (optional)

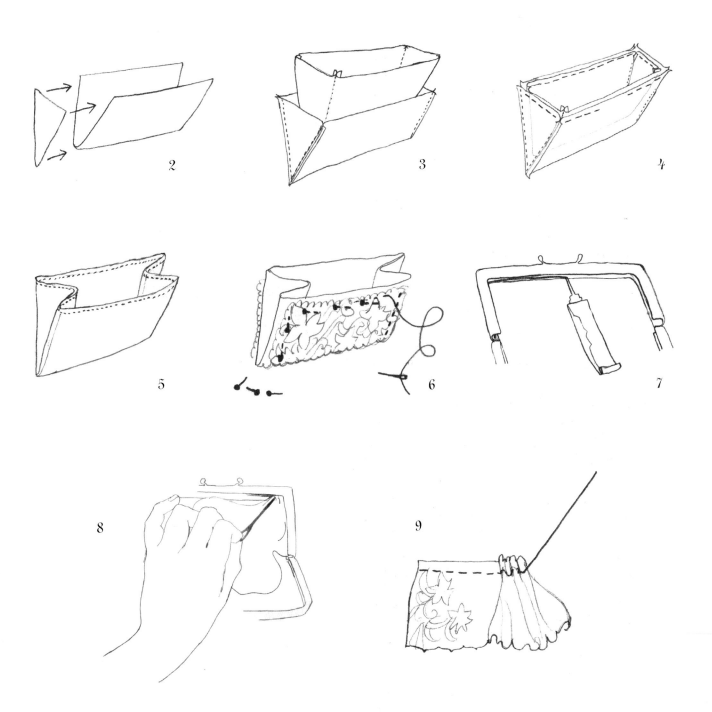

2

3

4

5

6

7

8

9

# Handkerchief Tablecloth

Not many people use delicate handkerchiefs nowadays; they seem quaint and slightly impractical with their lacy edges and ultra-fine cotton centres. The ones used to make this small tablecloth were in a pile of linen I inherited from a talented and prolific stitcher, and were all made by hand.

**MATERIALS**

Lace handkerchiefs

Iron

Pins

Needle

Matching sewing thread

Scissors

**INSTRUCTIONS**

1. Wash and carefully iron the handkerchiefs.

2. Lay the handkerchiefs out side by side on a large flat surface, then move them around to create a design you are happy with. Once this is done, pin the edges together to hold them in place.

3. Sew the handkerchiefs together using slipstitch, making sure the edges barely overlap. Repeat until all the edges have been stitched together, then press.

**TIP:** If the handkerchiefs you are using are extremely delicate, think about adding a backing fabric to provide a bit of strength – but use something fine such as chiffon or organza – and consider choosing a contrasting colour that will highlight the fragile lace edgings.

2

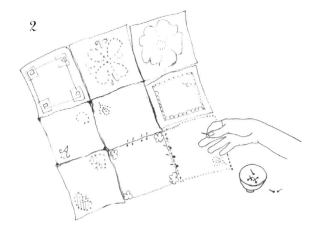

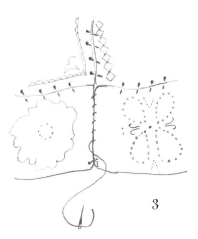

3

# Pompom Cushion

This project is a good way of reusing old knitwear, by boil-washing a pure wool jumper so that it shrinks and the fabric felts, then cutting it up to make a snuggly cushion. For extra decoration, add a tweed flower motif and have fun making woollen pompoms (see photograph overleaf).

(see photograph overleaf)

### INSTRUCTIONS

1. Boil-wash the jumper to give a felted appearance. You can do this by putting it through the hottest cycle on your washing machine. When it is dry, cut the jumper into two squares to fit your cushion pad, adding a 1.5cm (⅝in) seam allowance on all sides.

2. With right sides facing, pin and sew together three sides of the cushion cover using running stitch. Turn the cover right side out.

3. Trace the petal motifs on page 91 onto card, and cut out 4 large and 4 small petal motifs from the tweed fabric.

4. Using running stitch, attach each petal to the cushion to make a flower, leaving a space in the centre to attach the pompom.

5. Trace the pompom template on page 91 onto card twice, and cut around the outside and inside circles of each to create two rings.

6. Place the two pompom templates together, cut long lengths of wool and wind them around the template rings, binding them together. Continue adding lengths of wool, mixing in different colours, until the hole in the centre is full.

7. Using a pair of sharp scissors, cut around the outer edge of the pompom, inserting the tip of the scissors between the two pieces of card and using these as a guide.

8. Once you have cut all the way round, secure the loose wool threads by winding a length of wool between the two pieces of card and pulling it tightly around the centre of the threads. Tie in a double knot.

9. Plait together three lengths of wool and tie them around the centre of the pompom as before. Pull off the card templates, fluff up the pompom and use scissors to trim any loose or messy ends.

10. Repeat steps 6–9 to make another pompom. Then make one more pompom, but this time remove the template at step 8 and don't add a plaited cord.

11. Attach this last pompom to the centre of the flower motif, stitching it in place with a needle and thread. Sew the loose ends of the plaited cords of the other two pompoms to its base so that they appear to dangle from it (see photograph overleaf).

12. Insert the cushion pad into the cover and, using slipstitch and with the seam allowance tucked under, sew neatly along the open edge to close the cover.

## MATERIALS

100% wool jumper

Cushion pad

Tape measure

Scissors

Pins

Needle

Sewing thread

Tracing paper

Card (for pompom templates)

Tweed fabric

Assorted wool

1

2

4

6

7

8

9

# Templates

FLORAL JEANS PATCH,
PAGE 26

FLORAL APPLIQUÉ,
PAGE 54

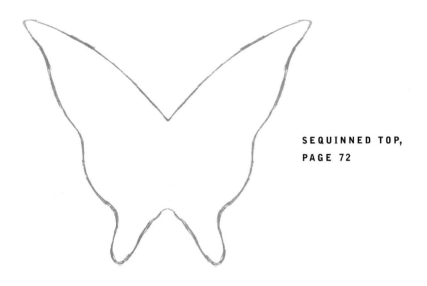

SEQUINNED TOP,
PAGE 72

POMPOM CUSHION PETALS
AND POMPOM, PAGE 86

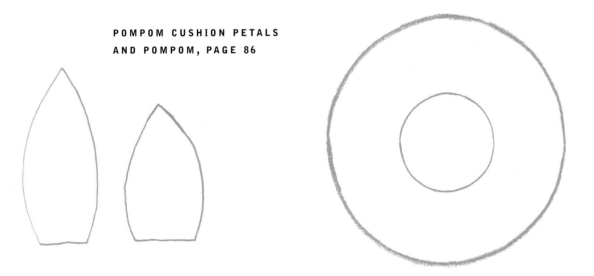

# Addresses

**ABBOTT & BOYD**

1/22 Chelsea Harbour Design Centre,
London, SW10 0XE
020 7351 9985
Designer furnishing fabrics for
upholstery, curtains, drapes, cushions
and pillows

**ANDREW MARTIN**

200 Walton Street, London, SW3 2LJ
020 7225 5100
www.andrewmartin.co.uk
Furnishing fabrics and trimmings

**ANNA FRENCH**

343 Kings Road, London, SW3 5ES
020 7351 1126
www.annafrench.co.uk
Range of modern and traditional
furnishing fabrics, lace and accessories

**ANTIQUE CRAFTS**

276 West Wycombe Road,
High Wycombe, Bucks, HP12 4AB
01494 447514
www.antiquecrafts.co.uk
Mail-order supplier of craft products,
offering a huge range of buttons, lace,
beads, embellishments and trimmings

**BARNYARNS**

Canal Wharf, Bondgate Green,
Ripon, North Yorkshire, HG4 1BR
0870 870 8586
www.barnyarns.com
Extensive sewing and embroidery
mail-order supplies

**THE BEAD SHOP**

21a Tower Street,
London, WC2H 9NS
020 7240 0931

www.beadworks.co.uk
All types of beads, including
semi-precious stones

**THE BERWICK STREET
CLOTH SHOP**

14 Berwick Street, London, W1F 0PP
020 7287 2881
Comprehensive range of fabrics
from wool to silk

**BOGOD MACHINE COMPANY**

Bogod House, 50–2 Great Sutton
Street, London, EC1V 0DJ
020 7253 1198
For sewing machines, overlockers
and accessories

**THE BUTTON QUEEN**

19 Marylebone Lane,
London, W1V 2NF
020 7935 1505
www.thebuttonqueen.co.uk
Every type of button you can
imagine and more!

**CATH KIDSTON**

51 Marylebone High Street,
London, W1U 5HW
020 7935 6555
Mail order: 020 7229 8000
www.cathkidston.co.uk
Furnishing fabrics and oilcloths

**COATS CRAFTS**

PO Box 22, Lingfield Point,
McMullen Road, Darlington,
Co. Durham, DL1 1YQ
01325 394237
www.coatscrafts.co.uk
For machine embroidery and
sewing threads

**CRAFT DEPOT**

Somerton Business Park,
Somerton, Somerset, TA11 6SB
01458 274727
www.craftdepot.co.uk
Mail-order craft supplies

**CRAFTMISTRESS**

66 Green Lane, Ockbrook,
Derby, DE27 3SE
01332 678945
www.craftmistress.co.uk
Embroidery and sewing products

**CRAFTY RIBBONS**

3 Beechwood Clump Farm,
Tin Pot Lane, Blandford,
Dorset, DT11 7TD
01258 455889
www.craftyribbons.com
Ribbon emporium

**DESIGNERS GUILD**

267 & 277 Kings Road,
London, SW3 5EN
020 7351 5775
www.designersguild.com
Modern interiors textiles,
upholstery and soft furnishings

**G J BEADS**

Court Arcade, The Wharf,
St Ives, Cornwall, TR26 1LG
01736 793886
www.gjbeads.co.uk
Mail-order beading supplies

**HOBBY CRAFT**

Forbury Retail Park, Off Kenavon
Drive, Reading, Berkshire, RG1 3HS
0118 902 8600
For store locations call:

0800 027 2387
www.hobbycraft.co.uk
Craft materials and equipment

**HOME CRAFTS DIRECT**
0116 269 7733
www.homecraftsdirect.co.uk
Mail-order craft materials

**IAN MANKIN**
109 Regents Park Road,
London, NW1 8UR
020 7722 0997
Mail order: 020 7722 0997
Includes good range of linen, cottons,
tickings, stripes and checks

**JENNIFER GAIL THREADS**
Studio, 1–3 Poole Hill,
Bournemouth, Dorset, BH2 5PW
01202 314144
www.jgthreads.com
Extensive range of space-dyed threads
and fabrics for embroidery, patchwork
and all textile art or craft

**JOHN LEWIS**
278–306 Oxford Street,
London, W1A 1EX
020 7629 7711
www.johnlewis.com
Fashion and furnishing fabric
department and good haberdashery.
Check the website for store locations

**LAURA ASHLEY**
256–8 Regent Street,
London, W1L 5DA
020 7437 9760
For a catalogue call: 08712 302301
www.lauraashley.com
Varied range of soft-furnishing fabrics

**LIBERTY**
Regent Street, London, W1B 5AH
020 7734 1234
www.liberty.co.uk
Dress and furnishing fabric
departments, plus embroidery
threads and trimmings

**MALABAR**
31–3 The South Bank
Business Centre, Ponton Road,
London, SW8 5BL
020 7501 4200
www.malabar.co.uk
Furnishing fabrics available
worldwide through interior
designers and retail outlets

**OSBORNE & LITTLE**
304 Kings Road, London, SW3 5UH
020 7352 1456
www.osborneandlittle.com
Leading designer of traditional
furnishing fabrics and wallpapers

**PONGEES**
28–30 Hoxton Square,
London, N1 6NN
020 7739 9130
www.pongees.co.uk
Specialize in silk and offer a huge
range; mail-order service available

**RAINBOW MAIL ORDER SILKS**
6 Wheelers Yard, High Street,
Great Missenden, Buckinghamshire,
HP16 0AL
01494 862111
www.rainbowsilks.co.uk
Stockists and mail-order suppliers
of a huge range of products for
embroidery and textile art and crafts,
including dyes, silks, velvets, paints
and dissolvable fabrics

**ROWAN YARNS**
Green Mill Lane, Holmfirth,
West Yorkshire, HD9 2DX
01484 681881
www.knitrowan.com
Comprehensive range of beautiful
natural yarns

**SHOREHAM KNITTING
& NEEDLECRAFT**
19 East Street, Shoreham-by-Sea,
West Sussex, BN43 5ZE
01273 461029
www.englishyarns.co.uk
Online yarn and thread store

**THE VOIRREY EMBROIDERY
CENTRE**
Brimstage Hall, Brimstage,
Wirral, CH63 6JA
0151 3423514
www.voirrey.com
Textile, needlework and knitting
stockists and mail-order suppliers

**V V ROULEAUX**
6 Marylebone High Street,
London, W1M 3PB
020 7224 5179
Huge range of trimmings in every
imaginable fabric and colourway

**WHALEYS**
Harris Court, Great Horton,
Bradford, West Yorkshire, BD7 4EQ
01274 576718
www.whaleys-bradford.ltd.uk
Stock includes utility fabrics, silks,
linen and jutes

# Index

# Acknowledgments

A big thank you to everyone who has worked on *Make Do & Mend*, especially the team at Conran Octopus – Zia Mattocks, Lucy Gowans, Siobhán O'Connor, Nicky Barneby, Jonathan Christie and Angela Couchman; to Chris Tubbs for his great pictures, speed, humour and good company, and his lovely assistant Natasha. Thank you also to Alice Tait for the beautiful illustrations and the hours spent locked in a room with the ever-patient Zia, trying to get their heads around all the projects in this book.